The Synaptic Archive

Decoding the Grid of Past Experiences in Present Minds

Milo Law

The Synaptic Archive

Chapter 1: The Architecture of Memory

Neural Storage Systems

The human brain orchestrates an intricate dance of electrical impulses and chemical signals, creating a vast network where memories take root and flourish. Within the dense forest of neurons, each connection serves as a potential storage unit, ready to capture and preserve the essence of our experiences. These neural storage systems operate with remarkable efficiency, utilizing specialized mechanisms to process, store, and maintain the countless pieces of information we encounter daily.

At the core of memory storage lies the hippocampus, a seahorse-shaped structure that acts as the primary gateway for new memories. Like a sophisticated filing system, it temporarily holds incoming information before determining its long-term significance. The process begins when sensory inputs trigger specific neural pathways, creating distinct patterns of activity that represent different aspects of an experience.

The storage mechanism relies heavily on synaptic plasticity, where connections between neurons strengthen or weaken based on their usage patterns. When we encounter meaningful information, neurons fire together in specific sequences, following Hebb's principle: neurons that fire together, wire together. This strengthening of neural pathways forms the physical basis of memory storage, creating robust networks that can persist for years or even decades.

The brain employs multiple storage formats, each optimized for different types of information. Procedural memories, such as riding a bicycle or typing on a keyboard, are stored in motor areas and the cerebellum. These memories form through repeated practice, gradually building stronger neural circuits that allow for automatic execution. Meanwhile, declarative memories, including facts and events, are processed through the temporal lobe and distributed across various cortical regions.

Emotional experiences receive special treatment in neural storage systems. The amygdala, an almond-shaped structure deep within the brain, tags memories with emotional significance, creating stronger and more vivid imprints. This explains why emotionally charged memories often feel more vivid and accessible than routine experiences. The system prioritizes survival-relevant information, ensuring quick access to memories that might be crucial for future decision-making.

The storage process involves multiple stages of consolidation. Initially, short-term storage holds information in an active state through continued neural firing patterns. During sleep and quiet moments, these temporary patterns undergo transformation into more stable, long-term formats. This process involves complex molecular changes at synapses, including protein synthesis and structural modifications that create lasting physical changes in the neural network.

Memory storage systems also implement sophisticated compression mechanisms. Rather than storing every detail of an experience, the brain extracts essential patterns and relationships, creating efficient representations that capture the meaning while discarding unnecessary details. This selective storage allows for better organization and retrieval of information while optimizing the use of neural resources.

The durability of stored memories varies significantly. Some memories become virtually permanent through a process called reconsolidation, where accessing a memory creates an opportunity to strengthen its neural foundations. Others gradually fade as neural pathways weaken from disuse or are modified by new experiences. This dynamic nature of storage ensures that the system remains adaptive, capable of updating and revising stored information based on new learning.

Redundancy plays a crucial role in neural storage systems. Important memories often distribute across multiple brain regions, creating backup copies that enhance reliability and resistance to damage. This distributed storage explains why memories can survive despite localized brain injury, as the system can often reconstruct information from remaining copies.

Age influences the efficiency of neural storage systems. Young brains exhibit heightened plasticity, allowing for rapid formation of new memories and easy modification of existing ones. As we age, these systems become more stable but less flexible, requiring more effort to encode new information while maintaining strong access to well-established memories.

Understanding neural storage systems reveals the remarkable complexity of human memory. Each moment of experience triggers cascading processes that determine what information becomes preserved and how it integrates into existing knowledge networks. The brain's ability to maintain vast amounts of information while constantly updating and refining its contents demonstrates the sophistication of these biological storage mechanisms.

The interplay between different storage systems creates a rich tapestry of memory, where facts, skills, emotions, and experiences weave together to form our personal history. This intricate organization allows us to navigate the present while maintaining connection with our past, supporting both immediate needs and long-term learning. Through continuous refinement and adaptation, neural storage systems maintain the delicate balance between stability and flexibility that characterizes human memory.

Memory Encoding Protocols

The transformation of experiences into stored memories follows precise biological protocols that orchestrate a complex interplay of neural mechanisms. These encoding processes determine what information becomes preserved and how it integrates into our existing knowledge framework. Like a sophisticated recording system, the brain employs multiple channels to capture different aspects of experience simultaneously.

Sensory information first enters through specialized receptors, triggering precise patterns of neural activity. Visual details activate specific regions in the occipital cortex, while auditory information flows through temporal areas. These separate streams of information undergo initial processing in their respective regions before converging in association areas where the brain begins to construct unified representations of experiences.

The encoding process heavily relies on attention mechanisms that act as gatekeepers, determining which aspects of experience receive priority processing. When we actively focus on specific details, the prefrontal cortex enhances the neural signals representing those elements, increasing their likelihood of successful encoding. This selective attention explains why we often remember details we specifically focused on while missing others that occurred simultaneously.

Emotional states significantly influence encoding strength. When experiences carry emotional weight, the amygdala releases neurochemical signals that enhance encoding processes across multiple brain regions. This mechanism explains why emotionally charged moments often become our most vivid and enduring memories. The brain essentially tags these experiences as particularly significant, allocating additional resources to their preservation.

The hippocampus plays a crucial role in binding different aspects of experience together during encoding. It creates temporal markers and spatial contexts, weaving separate elements into coherent episodes. This binding process allows us to later recall not just isolated facts but complete experiences with their associated contexts, emotions, and sensory details.

Pattern recognition mechanisms actively search for meaningful relationships during encoding. When new information aligns with existing knowledge, the brain creates stronger connections, facilitating both storage and future retrieval. This process of relating new information to established knowledge structures forms the basis of effective learning and memory formation.

Time stamps become automatically embedded during encoding, creating a temporal framework that helps organize memories chronologically. The brain maintains this temporal ordering through specialized neural circuits that track the sequence of events, allowing us to later reconstruct when specific experiences occurred relative to others.

The encoding process operates at multiple levels simultaneously. While conscious attention focuses on specific aspects, unconscious mechanisms continue processing background information, creating a rich contextual framework for each memory. This multilayered approach ensures that memories contain both focal points and supporting details that can aid future recall.

Physical state influences encoding effectiveness. Factors such as stress levels, fatigue, and arousal state can either enhance or impair the encoding process. Moderate stress can sharpen attention and strengthen encoding, while extreme stress might interfere with normal processing, leading to fragmented or incomplete memory formation.

The brain employs sophisticated compression algorithms during encoding, extracting essential patterns while discarding redundant information. This selective preservation helps maintain system efficiency while ensuring that crucial details remain intact. The process resembles data compression in digital systems but operates with remarkable biological precision.

Repetition and rehearsal during encoding create stronger memory traces. When information passes repeatedly through the same neural circuits, it strengthens the connections between involved neurons, increasing the likelihood of successful storage and future retrieval. This mechanism underlies the effectiveness of practice in learning new skills or information.

The encoding process also involves tagging memories with relevance markers that influence their accessibility. Experiences deemed important for survival, social interaction, or personal goals receive priority encoding, creating stronger and more readily accessible memory traces. This prioritization helps ensure that crucial information remains available when needed.

Chemical messengers play vital roles in modulating encoding strength. Neurotransmitters like dopamine and norepinephrine influence attention and arousal levels, while others affect the formation of stable neural connections. This chemical orchestra must maintain precise balance for optimal encoding to occur.

Understanding these encoding protocols reveals the sophisticated nature of memory formation. The brain's ability to rapidly process vast amounts of information while selecting and preserving what matters most demonstrates remarkable efficiency. These mechanisms ensure that our experiences transform into accessible memories that guide future behavior and shape our understanding of the world.

The encoding process represents the crucial first step in memory formation, determining what aspects of our experiences become part of our lasting mental archive. Through these carefully orchestrated protocols, the brain creates the foundation for all future memory operations, from storage to retrieval and integration.

Temporal Data Structures

Time flows through our memories like a river, carving channels and creating intricate patterns that shape how we store and access our experiences. The brain's temporal data structures form an elaborate framework that organizes memories along the dimension of time, creating a sophisticated system for maintaining chronological order and temporal relationships between events.

These temporal structures operate through specialized neural networks that timestamp experiences as they occur. Like a biological clock, neurons in the hippocampus and surrounding regions fire in specific patterns, marking each memory with its unique temporal signature. These timestamps become integral components of the memory itself, allowing us to later reconstruct when events occurred and their sequence relative to other experiences.

The organization of temporal data follows hierarchical patterns, with memories grouped into different time scales. Recent experiences maintain fine-grained temporal details, while older memories often compress into broader time periods. This hierarchical structure helps manage the vast amount of temporal information while maintaining efficient access to both recent and distant memories.

Temporal binding mechanisms link related events that occur across different time periods. When experiences share common elements or themes, the brain creates connections between their temporal markers, forming clusters of temporally related memories. These connections help us understand cause-and-effect relationships and recognize patterns that extend across time.

The precision of temporal coding varies with the significance of the experience. Highly emotional or important events often receive more detailed temporal markers, explaining why we can often pinpoint exactly when significant life events occurred while routine experiences blur together. This variable precision helps optimize the use of neural resources while preserving crucial temporal information.

Sequential ordering plays a vital role in temporal data structures. The brain maintains order through specialized neural circuits that encode the progression of events, creating chains of temporal associations. These sequences become particularly important for procedural memories, where the correct order of actions determines successful execution.

Time perception influences how temporal data becomes structured. During intense or novel experiences, time perception often slows, allowing for more detailed temporal encoding. Conversely, familiar or routine experiences may receive less detailed temporal markers, contributing to the sensation that time passes more quickly during mundane activities.

The brain employs sophisticated compression mechanisms for temporal data. Rather than storing every moment with equal detail, it creates reference points around significant events and interpolates the periods between them. This efficient coding system allows for flexible reconstruction of temporal sequences while minimizing storage requirements.

Temporal data structures also incorporate predictive elements. Based on past temporal patterns, the brain creates expectations about future events and their timing. These predictions help optimize attention and memory encoding, preparing neural systems for anticipated experiences at specific times.

The maintenance of temporal data involves continuous updating and refinement. As new experiences occur, temporal relationships shift and adjust, maintaining relative positions while accommodating new information. This dynamic nature ensures that temporal structures remain relevant and useful for current needs.

Sleep plays a crucial role in consolidating temporal data structures. During rest, the brain replays sequences of experiences, strengthening temporal associations and integrating new memories into existing chronological frameworks. This process helps stabilize temporal relationships and enhance their accessibility during wake periods.

The retrieval of temporal information relies on multiple access points. We can search our memories based on specific dates, relative time periods, or sequential relationships. This flexibility in temporal access allows us to navigate our memories from various perspectives, supporting both precise recall and broader historical understanding.

Emotional states influence temporal data organization. Strong emotions can create temporal anchors, points in time that serve as reference markers for surrounding events. These emotional timestamps often remain vivid long after the experience, helping structure our personal timelines.

The brain's temporal data structures demonstrate remarkable resilience. Even when specific details fade, the general temporal framework often persists, allowing us to maintain a sense of personal history and continuity. This preservation of temporal relationships supports our ability to learn from past experiences and plan for the future.

Understanding these temporal structures reveals the sophisticated nature of how our brains organize experiences in time. The intricate interplay between temporal coding, emotional significance, and memory consolidation creates a dynamic system that maintains our sense of personal history while supporting current needs and future planning.

The temporal dimension of memory provides essential context for our experiences, helping us navigate both past and future. Through these carefully structured temporal relationships, we maintain our connection to personal history while continuously adapting to new experiences and changing circumstances.

Experience Integration Networks

Deep within the brain's intricate architecture lies a remarkable system that weaves individual experiences into a cohesive tapestry of understanding. These networks function like master integrators, combining sensory inputs, emotional responses, and existing knowledge to create meaningful representations of our experiences.

The integration process begins the moment we encounter new information. As sensory signals arrive from different channels, specialized neural networks synchronize these inputs, creating unified percepts that represent the full richness of the experience. Visual, auditory, tactile, and other sensory information merge seamlessly, forming complete experiential records that capture the multifaceted nature of each moment.

Emotional circuits play a crucial role in this integration process. The amygdala and related structures evaluate the emotional significance of experiences, adding layers of meaning that color our perceptions and influence how memories form. These emotional tags become inseparable components of the integrated experience, affecting both its storage and future recall.

Prior knowledge significantly shapes how new experiences become integrated. Existing neural patterns serve as templates against which new information is compared and contextualized. When fresh experiences align with established patterns, integration occurs more smoothly, while novel or contradictory information may require the formation of new neural frameworks.

The hippocampus serves as a central hub for experience integration, binding different aspects of an event into coherent episodes. It creates temporal and spatial contexts that anchor experiences within our broader understanding, helping us make sense of when and where events occurred relative to other memories.

Integration networks operate across multiple time scales simultaneously. While immediate integration processes handle ongoing experiences, slower mechanisms work to incorporate new information into long-term knowledge structures. This multilayered approach ensures both rapid response to current situations and thoughtful adaptation of existing understanding.

Pattern recognition plays a vital role in experience integration. The brain constantly searches for similarities and relationships between new experiences and stored knowledge. These connections form the basis for learning and help us apply past experiences to novel situations, creating increasingly sophisticated understanding over time.

Social experiences receive special treatment in integration networks. Interactions with others trigger specialized neural circuits that process social cues, emotional responses, and interpersonal dynamics. These social integration mechanisms help us build complex models of human behavior and relationship patterns.

The brain employs sophisticated error-correction mechanisms during integration. When new experiences conflict with existing understanding, networks can initiate updates to stored knowledge, maintaining accuracy while preserving useful patterns. This dynamic balance between stability and adaptability ensures our mental models remain both reliable and current.

Sleep serves as a crucial period for experience integration. During rest, the brain replays and processes recent experiences, strengthening important connections and pruning unnecessary details. This consolidation process helps incorporate new information into existing knowledge structures while maintaining system efficiency.

Physical activities create unique integration patterns. Movement-based experiences engage motor circuits alongside sensory and cognitive networks, creating rich representations that include bodily states and spatial relationships. These integrated motor patterns form the foundation for skilled physical performance and spatial navigation.

The integration of experiences extends beyond mere combination of inputs. These networks actively generate predictions and expectations based on integrated knowledge, helping us anticipate future events and prepare appropriate responses. This predictive aspect of integration networks enhances our ability to navigate complex environments effectively.

Stress and emotional states significantly influence integration processes. Moderate stress can enhance integration by increasing attention and emotional tagging, while extreme stress may disrupt normal integration mechanisms, leading to fragmented or incomplete processing of experiences.

Learning and memory formation depend heavily on successful integration. When experiences become well-integrated, they form stronger memory traces and become more accessible for future use. This relationship between integration and learning efficiency explains why meaningful connections and context enhance our ability to remember and understand new information.

The flexibility of integration networks allows for continuous updating of our understanding. As we encounter new experiences, these networks modify existing patterns and create new connections, ensuring our knowledge remains adaptive and relevant. This dynamic nature supports lifelong learning and adaptation to changing circumstances.

Understanding these integration networks reveals the sophisticated nature of how we process and incorporate new experiences. Their ability to combine multiple sources of information while maintaining coherent and useful representations demonstrates the remarkable efficiency of biological information processing.

Through these carefully orchestrated integration mechanisms, our brains transform discrete experiences into meaningful knowledge that guides future behavior and shapes our understanding of the world. This continuous process of integration forms the foundation for learning, adaptation, and personal growth throughout our lives.

Memory Matrix Foundations

Memory exists as an intricate matrix of interconnected neural patterns, forming the fundamental architecture that supports all cognitive functions. This complex framework serves as the foundation upon which our experiences, knowledge, and skills are built, organized, and accessed.

The basic structure of the memory matrix emerges from patterns of synaptic connections between neurons. These connections form through precise chemical and electrical signals, creating vast networks that encode information through their specific arrangements and strengths. Like the foundation of a building, these neural patterns must be both stable enough to maintain information and flexible enough to accommodate new learning.

Each memory node within the matrix contains multiple components that work together to store different aspects of information. Sensory details, emotional contexts, temporal markers, and semantic meanings interweave to create rich, multidimensional memory representations. This layered structure allows for efficient storage and retrieval of complex information patterns.

The strength of connections within the memory matrix varies according to use and importance. Frequently accessed memories develop stronger neural pathways, while less-used connections may weaken over time. This dynamic strengthening and weakening process helps optimize the matrix for current needs while maintaining essential long-term memories.

Pattern completion mechanisms play a crucial role in the matrix structure. When partial information activates some components of a memory, these mechanisms can reconstruct the complete pattern by activating associated neural networks. This ability allows us to recall entire experiences from minimal cues, demonstrating the efficient organization of the memory matrix.

The matrix incorporates multiple levels of hierarchy, from simple sensory associations to complex abstract concepts. Lower levels handle basic pattern recognition and motor sequences, while higher levels manage sophisticated cognitive processes and conceptual understanding. These hierarchical layers work together seamlessly to support both simple and complex memory functions.

Emotional systems significantly influence matrix organization. The amygdala and related structures tag memories with emotional significance, creating stronger connections for experiences that carry emotional weight. These emotional markers become integral parts of the matrix structure, influencing how memories are stored and retrieved.

The spatial organization of memories within the matrix follows specific patterns. Related information tends to cluster together, creating neighborhoods of associated memories that can be accessed efficiently. This spatial arrangement helps optimize search processes and supports rapid retrieval of relevant information.

Time factors heavily into matrix structure through specialized temporal coding mechanisms. Recent memories maintain detailed temporal markers, while older memories often compress into more general time periods. This temporal organization helps maintain chronological relationships while managing storage efficiency.

The matrix foundation includes sophisticated error-correction mechanisms. When memories become degraded or corrupted, these systems can often reconstruct accurate information by referencing multiple related patterns. This redundancy helps maintain reliability while allowing for natural decay of less important details.

Sleep plays a vital role in maintaining and organizing the memory matrix. During rest periods, the brain actively strengthens important connections, prunes unnecessary ones, and reorganizes information patterns for optimal efficiency. This ongoing maintenance ensures the matrix remains both stable and adaptive.

Learning processes directly shape matrix structure through the formation of new connections and the modification of existing ones. As we acquire new knowledge or skills, the matrix reorganizes to incorporate this information while maintaining access to related existing memories. This dynamic restructuring supports continuous learning throughout life.

The matrix foundation includes specialized systems for different types of memories. Procedural memories, semantic knowledge, and episodic experiences each utilize distinct but interconnected matrix structures. These specialized systems work together to support the full range of memory functions while maintaining efficient organization.

Pattern recognition capabilities emerge from the matrix structure through the alignment of similar information patterns. When new experiences match existing patterns, they can quickly integrate into established matrix frameworks. This efficient integration process supports rapid learning and adaptation to familiar situations.

The stability of the memory matrix relies on biochemical processes that maintain neural connections over time. Protein synthesis and other molecular mechanisms work continuously to preserve important memory patterns while allowing for necessary modifications. This biological foundation ensures the longevity of essential memories.

Understanding the memory matrix reveals the sophisticated organization underlying our ability to store and access information. The intricate interplay between neural patterns, emotional markers, and temporal codes creates a dynamic system capable of supporting complex cognitive functions while maintaining efficiency and reliability.

The foundation of our memory system demonstrates remarkable resilience and adaptability. Through careful organization and continuous maintenance, the memory matrix provides the stable yet flexible infrastructure necessary for learning, remembering, and applying our experiences throughout life.

Chapter 2: Decoding Past Data

Memory Retrieval Mechanics

Memory retrieval operates through sophisticated neural mechanisms that orchestrate the recall of stored information with remarkable precision. The process begins when a trigger - whether internal thought or external stimulus - activates specific neural patterns associated with stored memories.

The hippocampus serves as the primary coordinator for memory retrieval, initiating a cascade of neural activities that spread across distributed brain regions. Like a conductor leading an orchestra, it synchronizes different brain areas to reconstruct the complete memory from its component parts stored throughout the cortex.

Pattern completion plays a crucial role in the retrieval process. When a partial memory cue activates some elements of a stored pattern, specialized neural circuits automatically fill in missing components. This completion mechanism explains why a familiar scent or song can suddenly trigger detailed recollections of past experiences.

The strength of memory traces significantly influences retrieval success. Memories reinforced through repeated recall or strong emotional associations develop robust neural pathways, making them easier to access. These well-worn neural paths act like frequently traveled roads, providing quick access to often-needed information.

Context plays a vital role in memory retrieval. Environmental cues, emotional states, and physical conditions similar to those present during memory formation can facilitate recall. This context-dependency explains why returning to a familiar place often triggers memories from previous visits.

Retrieval involves active reconstruction rather than simple playback. Each time we recall a memory, we essentially rebuild it using available cues and existing knowledge. This dynamic process can incorporate new information or perspectives, explaining why memories sometimes change slightly with each retrieval.

The speed and accuracy of retrieval depend on multiple factors. Recent memories generally retrieve more quickly than older ones, while emotionally significant memories often maintain their accessibility over time. The relevance of information to current needs also influences retrieval efficiency.

Memory interference can complicate retrieval processes. Similar memories may compete for activation, requiring additional neural mechanisms to select the most appropriate information. These competition resolution systems help maintain accuracy while managing the vast array of stored memories.

Stress levels significantly impact retrieval mechanics. Moderate stress can enhance retrieval by increasing attention and neural activation, while excessive stress may impair access to memories by disrupting normal hippocampal function. This relationship explains why stress can either help or hinder memory recall.

The brain employs sophisticated error-checking during retrieval. When recalled information seems inconsistent or incomplete, verification processes activate to cross-reference details with related memories and knowledge. This quality control helps maintain the accuracy of retrieved information.

Emotional states influence retrieval patterns through specialized neural circuits linking memory and emotion centers. Memories carrying strong emotional tags often retrieve more easily, particularly when current emotional states match those present during memory formation.

Sleep plays a crucial role in optimizing retrieval mechanisms. During rest, the brain consolidates important memories and strengthens retrieval pathways. This process explains why well-rested individuals often demonstrate better recall abilities than those who are sleep-deprived.

Age-related changes affect retrieval mechanics over time. While core retrieval processes remain intact throughout life, efficiency may decrease with age as neural connections naturally modify. However, frequent memory use helps maintain strong retrieval pathways even in later years.

The timing of retrieval attempts influences success rates. Spacing retrieval practice over time strengthens memory access paths more effectively than concentrated repetition. This spacing effect underlies effective learning strategies that distribute practice sessions across time.

Physical activity can enhance retrieval mechanics through increased blood flow and neural activation. Exercise promotes the release of chemicals that support neural function, potentially improving memory access and reconstruction processes.

Retrieval practice itself strengthens memory access paths. Each successful recall reinforces neural connections, making future retrieval attempts more efficient. This self-reinforcing aspect of memory retrieval explains why regular review enhances long-term retention.

The social context of retrieval can significantly impact success. Sharing memories with others often enhances recall through additional cues and perspectives provided by social interaction. This collaborative retrieval process can help uncover details that might otherwise remain inaccessible.

Understanding these retrieval mechanics reveals the complexity of memory access systems. The intricate interplay between neural activation patterns, emotional states, and environmental contexts creates a dynamic retrieval process that adapts to current needs while maintaining access to important information from our past.

The sophistication of memory retrieval mechanisms demonstrates the remarkable efficiency of biological information processing. Through these carefully orchestrated processes, we maintain access to our accumulated knowledge and experiences, supporting both immediate needs and long-term learning.

Timeline Integration Systems

Timeline integration systems operate as sophisticated neural mechanisms that organize and sequence our experiences across time, creating coherent narratives from discrete moments. These systems work continuously to place events in proper temporal order, establishing relationships between past experiences, present moments, and future predictions.

The hippocampus serves as the primary orchestrator of timeline integration, creating temporal stamps for experiences and maintaining their sequential relationships. Like a master chronicler, it weaves individual moments into continuous streams of experience, allowing us to understand how events relate to each other across time.

Temporal coding mechanisms embed specific time markers within memory traces. These markers help establish when events occurred relative to each other, creating a framework for organizing experiences chronologically. The precision of these temporal codes varies, with recent events typically carrying more detailed timing information than distant memories.

The brain maintains multiple parallel timelines at different scales. Short-term timelines track immediate sequences of events, while longer-term systems organize experiences across days, months, and years. These varying temporal scales work together to create a complete picture of our personal history.

Emotional significance influences timeline integration. Events carrying strong emotional weight often receive more prominent temporal markers, making them easier to locate within our personal chronology. This emotional tagging helps explain why significant life events often serve as reference points for organizing other memories.

Social interactions play a crucial role in timeline development. Shared experiences and collective memories help anchor personal timelines within broader social contexts. These social references strengthen temporal organization and provide additional cues for sequence reconstruction.

The integration of sensory information across time requires precise synchronization. Different aspects of an experience - visual, auditory, tactile - must align correctly to create coherent event representations. This temporal binding ensures that our memories accurately reflect the true sequence of sensory inputs.

Pattern recognition mechanisms help identify recurring temporal sequences. When similar patterns of events repeat, the brain creates temporal templates that aid in organizing and predicting future experiences. These templates support efficient processing of familiar temporal structures while remaining flexible enough to accommodate variations.

Sleep cycles significantly influence timeline integration. During rest, the brain processes recent experiences and incorporates them into existing temporal frameworks. This consolidation process helps maintain accurate chronological relationships while optimizing storage efficiency.

The prefrontal cortex plays a vital role in managing timeline complexity. It helps coordinate different temporal scales and resolve conflicts between competing temporal patterns. This executive control ensures that our sense of time remains coherent despite the complexity of our experiences.

Timeline integration systems demonstrate remarkable adaptability. They can compress or expand subjective time perception based on attention, emotion, and significance.

This flexibility allows for efficient processing of both rapid event sequences and extended time periods.

Memory consolidation processes continuously update timeline structures. As new experiences occur, they become integrated into existing temporal frameworks, sometimes causing slight adjustments to previously stored temporal relationships. This dynamic nature ensures our timeline remains both accurate and relevant.

Physical activities create distinct temporal patterns that influence timeline integration. Movement sequences, rhythmic activities, and spatial navigation all contribute to our understanding of temporal relationships. These embodied experiences help anchor abstract time concepts in concrete physical experiences.

The brain employs sophisticated error-correction mechanisms for timeline maintenance. When temporal information becomes degraded or confused, these systems can often reconstruct accurate sequences by referencing multiple related memories and contextual cues.

Cultural factors shape timeline integration through shared temporal frameworks. Calendars, schedules, and social rhythms provide external structures that help organize personal experiences within broader cultural contexts. These shared temporal references enhance communication and coordination of collective activities.

Timeline integration supports both retrospective and prospective thinking. By understanding how events relate across time, we can better reconstruct past experiences and anticipate future scenarios. This bidirectional temporal processing enables effective planning and decision-making.

The precision of timeline integration varies with attention and awareness. Mindful engagement with experiences tends to create stronger temporal markers, while automatic or habitual activities may receive less detailed temporal coding. This variation reflects the brain's efficiency in allocating processing resources.

Understanding timeline integration systems reveals the sophisticated nature of temporal organization in human cognition. These systems create the fundamental structure that allows us to navigate through time, learn from past experiences, and prepare for future events.

The complexity of timeline integration demonstrates the remarkable capabilities of biological information processing. Through these carefully orchestrated mechanisms, we maintain a coherent sense of temporal continuity while efficiently organizing vast amounts of experience-based information.

Experience Processing Algorithms

Experience processing unfolds through intricate neural algorithms that transform raw sensory inputs into meaningful memories and knowledge. These natural computational processes operate continuously, filtering, organizing, and integrating incoming information to create coherent representations of our experiences.

The initial stage of processing begins with parallel analysis of sensory streams. Visual, auditory, tactile, and other sensory inputs undergo rapid preliminary processing in specialized brain regions. These parallel processes extract key features and patterns from the raw sensory data, preparing it for higher-level integration.

Attention mechanisms play a crucial role by selecting which aspects of experience receive detailed processing. Like a sophisticated filter, these mechanisms enhance important signals while suppressing less relevant information. This selective processing ensures efficient use of neural resources while maintaining focus on significant aspects of experience.

Pattern matching systems continuously compare incoming information against stored knowledge. When new experiences align with existing patterns, they can be processed more efficiently. This comparative analysis helps identify familiar elements while highlighting novel aspects that require more detailed processing.

Emotional evaluation occurs automatically as experiences unfold. The amygdala and related structures rapidly assess the emotional significance of incoming information, tagging experiences with appropriate emotional markers. These emotional tags influence both immediate processing and long-term memory formation.

Context integration mechanisms weave together multiple aspects of an experience. Physical location, social situation, emotional state, and temporal factors combine to create rich contextual frameworks. These integrated contexts provide essential structure for understanding and remembering experiences.

The hippocampus coordinates the binding of different experience elements into cohesive episodes. This binding process ensures that various aspects of an experience - sensory details, emotions, thoughts, and actions - remain properly associated in memory. The resulting episodes form the building blocks of autobiographical memory.

Novelty detection systems identify unique or unexpected aspects of experiences. When encountered information differs significantly from predictions or stored patterns, these systems trigger enhanced processing. This heightened attention to novelty supports learning and adaptation to new situations.

Social processing algorithms analyze interpersonal aspects of experiences. These specialized systems interpret facial expressions, body language, vocal tones, and social contexts, creating rich representations of social interactions. This social processing significantly influences how experiences are understood and remembered.

Motor learning systems extract movement patterns from experiences. These systems identify successful action sequences and refine them through practice, gradually building sophisticated motor skills. The resulting procedural memories support efficient performance of complex physical tasks.

Semantic processing transforms concrete experiences into abstract knowledge. Through this process, specific instances become generalized concepts, supporting broader understanding and flexible application of learned information. This abstraction enables the transfer of knowledge across different contexts.

Time compression mechanisms condense extended experiences into manageable memory representations. While maintaining essential information, these processes optimize storage by summarizing repeated elements and highlighting significant changes. This efficient coding supports both detailed recall and general understanding.

Error correction operates continuously during experience processing. When inconsistencies arise between incoming information and existing knowledge, specialized mechanisms work to resolve these conflicts. This dynamic adjustment helps maintain accurate internal representations while accommodating new information.

Pattern completion systems fill in missing details during experience processing. When some aspects of an experience are unclear or incomplete, these systems use stored knowledge to generate reasonable predictions. This completion process helps create coherent representations despite incomplete information.

Consolidation processes continue to refine experience representations over time. During rest and sleep, the brain actively reorganizes and strengthens important aspects of recent experiences while allowing less significant details to fade. This ongoing processing optimizes memory storage and retrieval.

Cross-referencing mechanisms link related experiences together. By identifying common elements across different episodes, these processes create networks of associated memories. These connections support flexible thinking and creative problem-solving.

Prediction systems continuously generate expectations based on processed experiences. These predictions help prepare appropriate responses to anticipated situations while enabling quick detection of unexpected events. This predictive processing supports efficient adaptation to changing circumstances.

The sophistication of experience processing reveals the remarkable capabilities of biological information systems. Through these carefully orchestrated algorithms, raw sensory data transforms into meaningful experiences that guide behavior and support learning throughout life.

Understanding these natural processing mechanisms provides insight into how we make sense of our world. The complex interplay between attention, emotion, memory, and learning creates a dynamic system capable of extracting meaning from the continuous stream of experience.

Chapter 3: The Grid Framework

Memory Pattern Recognition

Memory pattern recognition operates as a fundamental cognitive process that enables us to identify, categorize, and respond to familiar elements within our ongoing experiences. This sophisticated neural mechanism forms the backbone of learning and adaptive behavior, allowing us to navigate complex environments with increasing efficiency.

The brain's pattern recognition system begins its work at the most basic sensory level, identifying simple recurring features in our environment. These foundational patterns might be specific shapes, sounds, or tactile sensations that frequently appear in our daily experiences. As these basic patterns combine, they form increasingly complex recognition templates.

Neural networks in the temporal lobe specialize in detecting and storing these recurring patterns. Like expert archaeologists piecing together fragments of ancient artifacts, these networks identify meaningful relationships between different elements of our experiences. The more frequently certain patterns occur, the stronger their neural representations become.

Pattern recognition in memory extends beyond simple sensory matching. It encompasses complex behavioral sequences, emotional responses, and abstract concepts. When you encounter a situation similar to a past experience, your brain rapidly activates relevant pattern templates, preparing appropriate responses based on previous outcomes.

The hippocampus plays a crucial role in pattern separation and completion. Pattern separation helps distinguish between similar but distinct experiences, while pattern completion allows us to recognize familiar situations even when we only encounter partial cues. This dual process ensures both precision and flexibility in pattern recognition.

Emotional states significantly influence pattern recognition processes. Patterns associated with strong emotional experiences often receive preferential processing, making them easier to recognize in future encounters. This emotional tagging helps prioritize important patterns that might be crucial for survival or well-being.

Context sensitivity shapes how patterns are recognized and interpreted. The same basic pattern might carry different meanings depending on its surrounding context, requiring sophisticated neural mechanisms to maintain appropriate flexibility in pattern recognition. This contextual processing ensures accurate interpretation of ambiguous patterns.

Social interactions create particularly complex patterns that require specialized recognition systems. These systems track recurring elements in human behavior, facial expressions, and social dynamics, helping us navigate interpersonal relationships more effectively. The ability to recognize social patterns contributes significantly to emotional intelligence.

Pattern recognition improves with experience through a process of continuous refinement. Each encounter with a familiar pattern strengthens relevant neural connections while slightly modifying the stored template to accommodate variations. This adaptive process allows pattern recognition to become increasingly sophisticated over time.

Sleep plays a vital role in consolidating and organizing pattern recognition templates. During rest, the brain processes recent experiences, extracting common patterns and integrating them with existing knowledge. This nocturnal processing enhances pattern recognition efficiency for future encounters.

The prefrontal cortex helps manage pattern recognition by providing executive oversight. It helps resolve conflicts between competing patterns and adjusts recognition sensitivity based on current goals and context. This top-down control ensures that pattern recognition serves our broader behavioral objectives.

Motor patterns receive special treatment in recognition systems. Physical activities create distinct neural signatures that, through repetition, become increasingly automatic. This specialization in motor pattern recognition supports the development of complex physical skills and habits.

Pattern recognition extends into temporal domains, identifying recurring sequences of events. These temporal patterns help us anticipate future occurrences and prepare appropriate responses in advance. The ability to recognize time-based patterns supports effective planning and decision-making.

Cultural exposure shapes pattern recognition capabilities. Different cultural environments emphasize different patterns, leading to enhanced recognition of culturally relevant features. This cultural influence demonstrates the flexibility of pattern recognition systems in adapting to varied environmental demands.

Learning environments can significantly impact pattern recognition development. Rich, varied experiences provide more opportunities for pattern discovery, while limited exposure may restrict pattern recognition capabilities. This relationship highlights the importance of diverse experiences in cognitive development.

Pattern recognition serves as a fundamental mechanism for knowledge transfer. When we encounter new situations, we automatically search for familiar patterns that might guide our responses. This pattern-based approach to novel situations supports efficient learning and problem-solving.

The sophistication of memory pattern recognition reveals the remarkable capabilities of biological information processing. Through these carefully orchestrated mechanisms, we transform raw experiences into meaningful patterns that guide our understanding and behavior.

Understanding these pattern recognition processes provides insight into how we learn from experience. The complex interplay between sensory processing, memory formation, and pattern matching creates a dynamic system capable of adapting to diverse challenges while maintaining efficient processing of familiar situations.

Emotional Data Indexing

Emotional data indexing operates as a sophisticated neural filing system that organizes experiences based on their emotional significance and characteristics. This intricate process ensures that emotionally relevant information remains accessible and influential in future decision-making and behavior.

The amygdala serves as the primary emotional indexing center, rapidly evaluating incoming experiences and tagging them with appropriate emotional markers. These markers act like digital timestamps, encoding both the type and intensity of emotional responses associated with specific memories. Through this process, experiences become cataloged within our emotional framework for future reference.

Positive emotions create distinct indexing patterns that differ from negative ones. Joy, love, and excitement generate markers that encourage approach behaviors, while fear, anger, and sadness create avoidance-oriented indices. This binary classification system helps optimize quick decision-making in similar future situations.

The hippocampus works in concert with the amygdala to bind emotional tags to specific contextual details. This collaboration ensures that emotional memories include relevant environmental, social, and temporal information. The resulting indexed memories provide rich, emotionally-informed guidance for navigating similar situations.

Social interactions receive particularly detailed emotional indexing. The brain maintains sophisticated records of emotional experiences involving others, creating complex webs of association that influence future social behavior. These social-emotional indices help us navigate relationships and interpret others' emotional states.

Stress hormones play a crucial role in emotional indexing strength. High-stress situations typically receive stronger emotional markers, making these memories more accessible and influential. This prioritization system ensures that potentially important survival information remains readily available.

The prefrontal cortex provides executive oversight of emotional indexing, helping to moderate and contextualize emotional associations. This top-down control prevents emotional indices from becoming overly dominant while ensuring appropriate emotional weighting of experiences.

Emotional indices undergo regular updating through reconsolidation processes. When we recall emotionally tagged memories, the associated emotional markers can be modified based on new experiences or perspectives. This flexibility allows our emotional filing system to remain current and relevant.

Sleep plays a vital role in organizing and consolidating emotional indices. During rest, the brain processes recent emotional experiences, strengthening important connections while allowing less significant emotional associations to fade. This nocturnal processing optimizes emotional memory organization.

Pattern recognition mechanisms identify recurring emotional themes across different experiences. These emotional patterns form higher-level indices that help us recognize and respond to similar emotional situations more effectively. The resulting emotional templates guide our interactions and decisions.

Cultural factors influence emotional indexing through shared emotional frameworks. Different cultures may emphasize different emotional aspects of experiences, leading to varied indexing patterns. This cultural shaping of emotional organization demonstrates the system's adaptability to social learning.

Physical sensations receive emotional tags that influence future bodily responses. The brain creates detailed indices linking emotional states with associated physical feelings, supporting both emotional recognition and regulation through bodily awareness.

Time perception interacts significantly with emotional indexing. Strongly emotional experiences often receive more detailed temporal markers, making them easier to locate within our personal timeline. This temporal-emotional binding supports accurate autobiographical memory.

Learning environments can significantly impact emotional indexing development. Supportive, emotionally rich environments tend to produce more nuanced and adaptive emotional indices, while adverse conditions may lead to oversimplified or maladaptive emotional tagging.

The precision of emotional indexing varies with attention and awareness. Mindful engagement with emotional experiences tends to create more accurate and useful emotional markers, while automatic or habitual responses may receive less detailed indexing.

Emotional indices serve as powerful retrieval cues for memory access. When we experience particular emotions, related memories become more accessible through their emotional tags. This association network supports emotional learning and decision-making.

The sophistication of emotional data indexing reveals the remarkable capabilities of biological information processing. Through these carefully orchestrated mechanisms, we maintain a dynamic emotional filing system that guides behavior and supports psychological well-being.

Understanding these emotional indexing processes provides insight into how we organize and learn from emotional experiences. The complex interplay between emotion, memory, and behavior creates a system capable of adapting to diverse emotional challenges while maintaining efficient processing of familiar situations.

The development of healthy emotional indexing patterns plays a crucial role in psychological resilience. By maintaining flexible and appropriate emotional associations, we can better navigate life's challenges while building meaningful relationships and experiences.

Neural Network Connections

Neural network connections form the fundamental architecture of information processing in biological systems, creating intricate pathways that enable learning, memory, and behavior. These connections, known as synapses, number in the trillions, forming dynamic patterns that constantly evolve through experience and adaptation.

The formation of neural connections begins during early development, following genetic blueprints that establish basic brain architecture. As experiences accumulate, these initial connections undergo extensive refinement through processes of strengthening, weakening, creation, and elimination. This remarkable plasticity allows networks to optimize their structure for specific functions.

Synaptic strength plays a crucial role in network operation. Strong connections facilitate reliable information transmission, while weaker ones provide flexibility for future modification. The balance between connection stability and plasticity enables networks to maintain important memories while remaining adaptable to new information.

Neurotransmitters serve as chemical messengers at connection points, influencing how signals propagate through networks. Different neurotransmitter systems create varied effects on network function, allowing for complex modulation of information flow. This chemical diversity supports the wide range of mental processes necessary for cognition and behavior.

Network connections exhibit remarkable specificity in their organization. Neurons form precise patterns of connectivity based on both genetic guidance and activity-dependent refinement. This precise wiring ensures efficient information processing while minimizing resource consumption.

Learning processes modify network connections through several mechanisms. Hebbian plasticity strengthens connections between neurons that fire together, while homeostatic processes maintain overall network stability. These complementary mechanisms enable effective learning while preventing runaway excitation or inhibition.

The spatial arrangement of connections influences network function. Local connections support detailed processing within brain regions, while long-range connections enable integration across distant areas. This hierarchical organization allows for both specialized processing and global coordination.

Time plays a crucial role in connection dynamics. The timing of signals arriving at synapses affects how connections change, with precise timing differences leading to different modifications. This temporal sensitivity enables networks to encode complex temporal patterns in their connection structure.

Sleep serves as a critical period for connection maintenance and refinement. During rest, networks undergo systematic modification, strengthening important connections while pruning unnecessary ones. This nocturnal maintenance optimizes network performance for subsequent wake periods.

Emotional states significantly influence connection modification. Strong emotions can trigger molecular cascades that enhance connection plasticity, leading to more robust memory formation. This emotional modulation helps prioritize significant experiences in network organization.

Social interactions create unique patterns of network activation and modification. Connections involved in social processing receive special attention during development and remain particularly plastic throughout life. This social specialization supports the sophisticated interpersonal abilities crucial for human behavior.

Physical activity impacts network connections through multiple mechanisms. Exercise increases factors that promote connection formation and maintenance, while motor learning creates specialized connection patterns. This physical influence demonstrates the intimate link between body and brain.

Environmental enrichment enhances network complexity through increased connection formation and refinement. Rich environments stimulate the creation of new connections while promoting the maintenance of existing ones. This environmental sensitivity allows networks to adapt to varying cognitive demands.

Stress can significantly affect network connections, potentially leading to both adaptive and maladaptive changes. Acute stress may enhance certain connections related to survival, while chronic stress often leads to connection loss. Understanding these effects helps explain stress-related cognitive changes.

Age-related changes in network connections follow distinct patterns throughout life. Early development sees rapid connection formation, followed by pruning and refinement. Later life typically involves gradual connection loss, though maintenance mechanisms can preserve crucial functions.

Network connection patterns show individual variation while maintaining core similarities across people. These individual differences arise from both genetic factors and unique life experiences. Understanding this variation helps explain individual differences in cognitive abilities and behavior.

The health of network connections depends on various biological factors. Proper nutrition, adequate sleep, and appropriate levels of physical activity all contribute to connection maintenance. These factors highlight the importance of lifestyle in supporting optimal network function.

Recovery processes can repair damaged network connections under certain conditions. While some damage may be permanent, networks often show remarkable ability to reorganize and compensate for losses. This adaptability provides hope for recovery from various brain injuries and conditions.

Understanding neural network connections reveals the remarkable complexity and adaptability of biological information processing. These connections form the basis of all mental functions, from simple reflexes to complex thoughts and emotions. Their proper maintenance and modification are crucial for cognitive health throughout life.

Chapter 4: Memory Processing Dynamics

Cognitive Compression Methods

Cognitive compression methods represent the brain's remarkable ability to efficiently store and process vast amounts of information through sophisticated encoding strategies. These natural compression techniques enable us to manage the constant influx of sensory data while maintaining quick access to essential information.

The brain employs several fundamental compression strategies, with chunking serving as a primary mechanism. Rather than storing individual bits of information separately, related elements are grouped into meaningful units. For instance, when remembering a phone number, we naturally group digits into chunks of three or four, making the sequence more manageable and easier to recall.

Pattern extraction forms another crucial compression method, where the brain identifies and stores common features across multiple experiences. Instead of maintaining complete records of every similar event, the brain preserves the essential patterns while discarding redundant details. This efficient storage system allows for quick recognition of familiar situations while minimizing cognitive load.

Hierarchical organization provides a powerful compression framework, where information is stored at different levels of abstraction. General concepts occupy higher levels, while specific details reside at lower levels. This structure allows for efficient storage and retrieval, as we can access broad categories quickly and drill down to specifics only when needed.

Emotional significance acts as a compression filter, helping determine which information receives detailed encoding and which can be stored in more compressed forms. Experiences with strong emotional content typically receive more detailed preservation, while emotionally neutral information often undergoes greater compression.

Spatial relationships offer another avenue for compression, as the brain leverages existing spatial understanding to organize and store information. This explains why spatial memory techniques, such as the method of loci, prove so effective for remembering sequences of information. The brain naturally compresses new information by linking it to familiar spatial frameworks.

Temporal compression occurs through the summarization of extended experiences into key moments or highlights. Rather than storing every detail of a lengthy event, the brain preserves critical points and transitions, creating a compressed timeline that captures the essence of the experience while minimizing storage requirements.

Context-based compression allows for efficient storage by maintaining links to relevant contextual frameworks rather than duplicating information. When similar information appears in different contexts, the brain stores the unique elements while referencing shared contextual details, significantly reducing storage overhead.

Sensory compression involves reducing the complexity of incoming sensory information while preserving essential features. The brain automatically filters out redundant or irrelevant sensory data, maintaining only the information necessary for understanding and responding to our environment.

Language serves as a powerful compression tool, allowing complex ideas and experiences to be encoded into concise symbolic representations. Through language, we can compress elaborate concepts into single words or phrases, enabling efficient storage and communication of complex information.

Motor skill compression occurs through the automation of movement sequences. Initially complex motor patterns become compressed into streamlined neural programs, requiring minimal conscious oversight. This compression of motor information allows for smooth, efficient execution of learned movements.

Social compression methods help manage the complexity of interpersonal interactions by identifying and storing common patterns in human behavior. Rather than maintaining detailed records of every social encounter, the brain compresses social information into representative models and scripts.

Memory reconsolidation provides opportunities for adaptive compression, as memories are modified and potentially further compressed each time they are recalled. This dynamic process allows for continuous optimization of information storage based on relevance and utility.

Schema-based compression leverages existing knowledge frameworks to efficiently store new information. Rather than encoding every detail of new experiences, the brain stores primarily the deviations from established schemas, significantly reducing storage requirements.

Predictive compression enables efficient processing by maintaining compressed models of expected outcomes. The brain stores primarily the differences between predictions and actual experiences, rather than complete representations of each new event.

Practice and repetition enhance compression efficiency by identifying and strengthening essential patterns while allowing irrelevant details to fade. This selective reinforcement leads to increasingly efficient storage of frequently accessed information.

The development of effective cognitive compression methods plays a crucial role in learning and expertise. As skills advance, practitioners develop increasingly sophisticated compression strategies specific to their domain of expertise, enabling rapid access to relevant information.

Understanding these natural compression methods provides insight into how we can optimize learning and memory processes. By working with rather than against these innate compression strategies, we can enhance our ability to acquire and retain new information while maintaining cognitive efficiency.

The sophistication of cognitive compression methods demonstrates the remarkable efficiency of biological information processing. These compression strategies enable us to navigate complex environments while maintaining quick access to essential information for survival and success.

Data Retrieval Optimization

Data retrieval optimization in biological systems represents a sophisticated interplay of neural mechanisms that enable rapid, accurate access to stored information. The brain's remarkable ability to quickly locate and retrieve relevant data from vast storage networks relies on multiple optimization strategies working in concert.

Memory traces strengthen through repeated activation, creating well-worn neural pathways that facilitate faster future retrieval. These optimized pathways function like frequently used shortcuts, allowing quick access to commonly needed information. The process resembles a city's transportation system, where major routes receive more maintenance and development to handle regular traffic efficiently.

Emotional salience serves as a powerful optimization factor, with emotionally significant memories receiving privileged access pathways. The amygdala's influence ensures that emotionally tagged information remains readily accessible, creating a natural prioritization system for potentially important data. This evolutionary adaptation ensures quick retrieval of survival-relevant information.

Context-dependent optimization allows for more efficient retrieval by maintaining strong associations between related pieces of information. When accessing one piece of data, related information becomes temporarily more accessible, similar to how opening one file on a computer might pre-load associated files for faster access.

The hippocampus plays a crucial role in optimization by creating detailed indices of experiences, allowing for rapid searching across multiple dimensions. These indices include spatial, temporal, and categorical markers that can be used simultaneously to locate specific memories, much like a sophisticated database search engine.

Sleep cycles actively contribute to retrieval optimization through memory consolidation and reorganization. During sleep, the brain strengthens important connections while pruning unnecessary ones, effectively defragmenting its storage system for more efficient future access. This process resembles regular maintenance on a complex filing system.

Physical activity enhances retrieval efficiency by increasing blood flow to key brain regions and promoting the production of factors that support neural plasticity. Regular exercise helps maintain optimal conditions for both storage and retrieval processes, much like keeping computer hardware in peak operating condition.

State-dependent optimization occurs when retrieval becomes more efficient under conditions similar to those present during initial storage. This phenomenon explains why returning to a specific location or emotional state can suddenly trigger related memories, providing an additional pathway for access.

Pattern completion mechanisms allow for efficient retrieval from partial cues, reducing the need for exact matches to access stored information. This flexibility enables quick recognition and recall even when presented with incomplete or degraded stimuli, similar to how a search engine can find relevant results from partial keywords.

Hierarchical organization optimizes retrieval by maintaining information at multiple levels of specificity. This structure allows for rapid navigation from general categories to specific details, much like clicking through folders on a computer to locate a particular file.

Social interaction enhances retrieval optimization through shared recall and collaborative memory processes. Group discussions often facilitate access to information that might be difficult to retrieve individually, demonstrating the power of networked retrieval systems.

Attention mechanisms play a vital role in optimization by directing cognitive resources toward relevant retrieval pathways while suppressing irrelevant ones. This focused approach prevents system overload and ensures more efficient access to desired information.

Stress levels significantly impact retrieval efficiency, with moderate stress potentially enhancing performance while extreme stress often impairs it. Understanding this relationship helps in creating optimal conditions for accessing stored information.

Regular review and retrieval practice strengthen access pathways through a process called retrieval-induced facilitation. Each successful retrieval attempt makes subsequent access easier, similar to how frequently used trails become clearer and more easily navigable.

Cross-referencing between different types of stored information creates multiple access routes to important data. These redundant pathways provide backup retrieval options when primary routes are temporarily unavailable or less efficient.

Time-based optimization occurs through the natural strengthening of significant memories and fading of less important ones. This automatic prioritization helps maintain efficient access to relevant information while reducing interference from non-essential data.

Environmental cues serve as powerful optimization tools, with specific surroundings often triggering rapid access to associated memories. This context-sensitivity helps explain why returning to familiar places can suddenly activate long-dormant memories.

The development of expertise in specific domains leads to highly optimized retrieval pathways for domain-relevant information. These specialized networks enable experts to quickly access complex information within their field of knowledge.

Understanding these optimization mechanisms provides valuable insights into improving personal information management and learning strategies. By working with these natural processes, we can enhance our ability to store and retrieve information effectively, supporting better decision-making and problem-solving capabilities.

Experiential File Management

Experiential file management encompasses the intricate processes through which the human brain organizes, categorizes, and maintains memories and experiences. Much like a sophisticated filing system, our minds create complex organizational structures that enable us to store and access life experiences efficiently.

The process begins with initial encoding, where experiences are filtered through attention and emotional significance. Meaningful events receive priority status in our mental filing system, while routine or less significant experiences may be stored in more compressed formats. This selective filing helps prevent overwhelming our cognitive resources while ensuring important information remains readily accessible.

Our experiential files are organized through multiple classification systems operating simultaneously. Temporal markers act as primary indexing tools, allowing us to locate experiences within our personal timeline. Spatial information provides another crucial filing dimension, linking memories to specific locations and environmental contexts. These multidimensional indexes enable flexible access to stored experiences from various entry points.

Emotional tagging serves as a powerful filing mechanism, creating distinct categories based on affective significance. Joy, fear, surprise, and other emotions act as specialized folders, allowing quick access to experiences sharing similar emotional qualities. This emotional classification system evolved to prioritize survival-relevant information but now serves broader purposes in our social and personal lives.

Social connections form another vital filing dimension, with experiences organized according to the people involved. Our brains maintain sophisticated relationship-based filing systems, allowing quick access to shared experiences and interpersonal histories. This social organization supports navigation of complex social networks and relationship maintenance.

The management system automatically updates and reorganizes files through regular maintenance processes. During sleep, recent experiences are consolidated and integrated with existing knowledge, while less relevant information may be archived or pruned. This ongoing optimization ensures efficient storage and retrieval while maintaining system flexibility.

Context-based cross-referencing creates multiple access pathways to stored experiences. A single event might be filed under various categories - location, participants, emotions, and outcomes - enabling retrieval through multiple routes. This redundancy provides robust access while supporting creative connections between different experiences.

The system employs hierarchical organization, with experiences filed at different levels of detail and abstraction. General patterns and principles occupy higher-level folders, while specific details reside in nested subfolders. This structure allows quick access to relevant information while maintaining the ability to drill down for details when needed.

Personal significance acts as a key filing criterion, with experiences organized according to their importance in our life narrative. Milestone events receive prominent placement, while routine experiences may be compressed or merged into representative summaries. This prioritization helps maintain an efficient yet meaningful personal history.

Learning experiences receive special treatment in the filing system, with successful problem-solving strategies and acquired skills stored in readily accessible formats. The system maintains links between related learning experiences, facilitating the transfer of knowledge across different contexts and situations.

Environmental triggers serve as external filing aids, with specific locations, sounds, or smells linked to stored experiences. These environmental connections create additional access routes to our experiential files, explaining why certain places or sensory inputs can suddenly activate detailed memories.

Regular review and reflection strengthen file organization by reinforcing important connections and updating relevance markers. Through conscious reflection, we can enhance the accessibility of valuable experiences and maintain better organization of our mental files.

The system demonstrates remarkable adaptability, reorganizing files based on new experiences and changing priorities. What seemed crucial at one point may be refiled as less important when circumstances change, while previously peripheral experiences might gain new significance.

Cultural frameworks influence file organization, with shared social meanings and values affecting how we categorize and interpret experiences. These cultural filing systems help us make sense of experiences within our social context while facilitating communication with others.

Professional expertise leads to specialized filing structures for domain-specific experiences. Experts develop refined categorization systems within their fields, enabling quick access to relevant knowledge and experience patterns.

Age-related changes affect file management processes, with older adults often showing different organization patterns than younger individuals. While some filing efficiency may decrease with age, experience-based organization often becomes more sophisticated.

The quality of our experiential file management significantly impacts decision-making and personal growth. Well-organized experiential files support better problem-solving by providing quick access to relevant past experiences and learned lessons.

Understanding these natural filing processes helps us work more effectively with our cognitive systems. By consciously supporting our brain's organizational tendencies, we can enhance our ability to learn from experiences and apply past knowledge to new situations. This improved management of experiential files contributes to better adaptation and personal development throughout life.

Chapter 5: The Integration Interface

Present-Past Synchronization

Present-past synchronization represents a fundamental cognitive process that bridges our current experiences with stored memories, creating a seamless integration of temporal information. This dynamic mechanism allows us to navigate present situations by drawing upon relevant past experiences while simultaneously updating our memory banks with new information.

The synchronization process operates continuously, comparing incoming sensory data with stored experiences to identify meaningful patterns and guide responses. When walking into a familiar restaurant, for instance, our brains rapidly sync current sensory inputs with previous dining experiences, helping us anticipate the sequence of events and appropriate behaviors.

Emotional resonance plays a crucial role in this synchronization, as current emotional states activate memories with similar affective signatures. This emotional bridging helps us understand present situations through the lens of past experiences while adding nuanced updates to our emotional memory database. The process explains why certain present moments can suddenly trigger vivid emotional memories from our past.

The hippocampus serves as a primary synchronization hub, rapidly comparing current experiences with stored memory traces to identify relevant matches and differences. This real-time comparison enables quick recognition of familiar patterns while highlighting novel elements that require attention and new learning.

Social interactions particularly benefit from present-past synchronization, as we constantly match current social cues with stored knowledge about human behavior. This rapid synchronization allows us to navigate complex social situations by drawing upon our accumulated understanding of social dynamics while incorporating new observations.

Environmental contexts trigger automatic synchronization processes, with current surroundings activating relevant spatial and contextual memories. This location-based syncing helps us quickly adapt to familiar environments while remaining alert to changes that might require updated responses.

Motor skills demonstrate present-past synchronization through the continuous refinement of movement patterns. Each execution of a familiar action, from writing to playing an instrument, involves syncing stored motor programs with current conditions while incorporating subtle adjustments for improved performance.

Learning processes rely heavily on effective present-past synchronization, as new information must be integrated with existing knowledge structures. The brain actively compares incoming information with stored concepts, creating updated understanding through this dynamic synchronization process.

Time perception itself emerges from successful present-past synchronization, as our sense of now constantly integrates with recent memory traces to create a coherent experience of temporal flow. This process explains why time seems to move differently depending on how effectively we sync current experiences with stored memories.

Problem-solving capabilities depend on rapid synchronization between current challenges and past solutions. When facing a new problem, our brains quickly search for relevant past experiences, synchronizing applicable elements while adapting strategies to current circumstances.

Language processing demonstrates present-past synchronization through the continuous matching of current linguistic input with stored language patterns. This enables rapid comprehension and appropriate responses while allowing for the incorporation of new linguistic information.

Skill development benefits from increasingly refined synchronization processes, as expertise grows through the progressive integration of new experiences with established knowledge. Expert performance often reflects highly efficient present-past synchronization in specific domains.

Stress can significantly impact synchronization efficiency, potentially disrupting the smooth integration of present experiences with relevant memories. Understanding this relationship helps in managing conditions for optimal cognitive performance.

Cultural frameworks influence synchronization patterns by shaping which elements of experience receive priority in the matching process. Cultural knowledge provides important templates for interpreting current situations through the lens of accumulated wisdom.

Age-related changes in synchronization processes can affect how effectively we integrate new experiences with stored memories. While processing speed may decrease, accumulated experience often provides richer templates for understanding present situations.

Sleep plays a vital role in maintaining effective synchronization by consolidating recent experiences and updating existing memory structures. This nighttime processing ensures better integration of new information with stored knowledge.

Physical activity enhances synchronization processes by improving neural plasticity and cognitive function. Regular exercise supports better integration of current experiences with stored memories while maintaining cognitive flexibility.

Mindfulness practices can strengthen present-past synchronization by increasing awareness of both current experiences and their connections to stored memories. This enhanced awareness supports more effective integration of new information with existing knowledge.

Understanding these synchronization mechanisms provides valuable insights for improving learning and performance. By consciously supporting natural synchronization processes, we can enhance our ability to learn from experience while maintaining adaptive responses to current situations.

The effectiveness of present-past synchronization significantly impacts our daily functioning, influencing everything from basic motor skills to complex social interactions. This fundamental cognitive process underlies our ability to navigate life's challenges while continuously updating our understanding of the world around us.

Memory Access Protocols

Memory access protocols operate as sophisticated neural mechanisms that govern how we retrieve and utilize stored information in our brains. These protocols function like intricate gatekeeping systems, determining which memories become accessible, when they surface, and how they integrate with current cognitive processes.

Primary access protocols rely on emotional salience, with the amygdala playing a crucial role in prioritizing emotionally significant memories. When we encounter situations that trigger strong feelings, these protocols rapidly activate relevant emotional memories, preparing us for appropriate responses. This evolutionary adaptation ensures quick access to survival-critical information while maintaining efficient processing of routine experiences.

Contextual cues serve as key access triggers, with environmental factors automatically activating associated memory protocols. Walking into your childhood home might instantly unlock a cascade of memories through these context-sensitive protocols. The hippocampus orchestrates this process, matching current sensory inputs with stored spatial and temporal markers.

Social interactions trigger specialized access protocols that retrieve relevant interpersonal memories and behavioral scripts. When meeting someone familiar, these protocols quickly activate stored information about previous encounters, shared experiences, and appropriate social responses. This rapid access supports smooth social navigation and relationship maintenance.

Time-based protocols organize memory access according to temporal relevance, with recent experiences generally receiving privileged access status. However, these protocols also maintain flexible access to older memories based on their significance and current relevance. The system continuously updates temporal markers to maintain efficient access patterns.

State-dependent protocols modify memory accessibility based on our current physical and psychological condition. Memories formed during similar states become more accessible, explaining why certain moods can trigger specific memory patterns. Understanding these protocols helps in creating optimal conditions for memory access when needed.

Learning-oriented protocols facilitate access to educational and skill-based memories through practice and repetition. These protocols strengthen access pathways to frequently used information while maintaining flexibility for updating and modification. Regular engagement with stored knowledge reinforces these access routes.

Pattern recognition protocols enable rapid access to relevant memories based on similarity matching. When encountering new situations, these protocols quickly scan stored experiences for useful patterns, supporting efficient problem-solving and decision-making. The process operates automatically but can be enhanced through conscious attention.

Motor memory protocols govern access to stored movement patterns, enabling smooth execution of learned physical skills. These protocols become increasingly refined through practice, allowing for automatic access to complex movement sequences while maintaining adaptability to current conditions.

Language processing protocols coordinate access to linguistic knowledge, enabling fluid communication through rapid retrieval of vocabulary, grammar, and contextual understanding. These protocols operate across multiple levels simultaneously, from individual word recognition to complex narrative comprehension.

Stress-response protocols modify memory access patterns during challenging situations, potentially enhancing access to relevant survival information while temporarily suppressing less critical memories. Understanding these protocols helps in managing stress-related memory effects.

Sleep-dependent protocols actively maintain and optimize memory access systems during rest periods. During sleep, the brain reorganizes access pathways, strengthening important connections while pruning unnecessary ones. This maintenance ensures efficient memory access during waking hours.

Expert-level protocols develop through extensive experience in specific domains, creating specialized access routes to domain-relevant information. These refined protocols enable experts to quickly access complex knowledge structures while maintaining flexibility for new learning.

Cross-referencing protocols enable access to memories through multiple pathways, creating redundant access routes for important information. This redundancy ensures reliable memory retrieval while supporting creative connections between different knowledge domains.

Attention-based protocols filter incoming information and direct cognitive resources toward relevant memory access pathways. These protocols help prevent system overload while maintaining focus on currently important information.

Age-related changes in access protocols can affect retrieval efficiency, though compensatory mechanisms often develop to maintain functional access to important memories. Understanding these changes helps in adapting memory strategies throughout life.

Cultural protocols influence memory access by providing shared frameworks for organizing and interpreting experiences. These culturally-shaped protocols affect which memories become easily accessible in different social contexts.

Physical activity enhances memory access protocols through improved neural circulation and plasticity. Regular exercise supports optimal functioning of these protocols while maintaining cognitive flexibility.

Mindfulness practices can refine memory access protocols by increasing awareness of retrieval processes and reducing interference from irrelevant thoughts. This enhanced awareness supports more efficient memory access and utilization.

Understanding these various memory access protocols provides valuable insights for optimizing personal cognitive function. By working with these natural mechanisms rather than against them, we can enhance our ability to access and utilize stored information effectively. These protocols form the foundation of our cognitive capabilities, supporting everything from basic survival skills to complex intellectual achievements.

Reality Construction Systems

Reality construction systems form the fundamental cognitive architecture through which our brains create our perception of the world. These intricate neural mechanisms transform raw sensory input into meaningful experiences, shaping our understanding of reality through multiple layers of processing and interpretation.

The foundation of reality construction begins with sensory integration, where diverse inputs from our eyes, ears, skin, and other sensory organs combine to create a coherent experience. This process occurs automatically, yet involves sophisticated filtering and prioritization mechanisms that determine which aspects of our environment receive conscious attention.

Personal history significantly influences how we construct reality, as past experiences create templates through which we interpret new information. When walking into a room, for instance, our brains rapidly construct meaning based not just on current sensory data, but on accumulated knowledge about similar spaces and situations.

Emotional systems play a crucial role in reality construction, coloring our perceptions with affective significance. A sunset isn't merely processed as patterns of light and color, but as an experience that might evoke feelings of peace, nostalgia, or wonder. These emotional overlays become integral parts of our constructed reality.

Social interactions particularly highlight the complexity of reality construction, as we simultaneously process verbal and non-verbal cues, interpret intentions, and navigate cultural norms. Our brains construct complex social realities by integrating multiple streams of information with stored knowledge about human behavior.

Environmental context shapes reality construction through both physical and psychological dimensions. The same physical space might be constructed differently in our minds depending on its purpose - a classroom feels different from a dining room, even with similar physical characteristics.

Memory systems actively participate in reality construction by providing historical context and expectations. Our constructed reality at any moment includes not just present sensory information, but projections based on past experiences and anticipated futures.

Cultural frameworks significantly influence reality construction by providing shared meanings and interpretations. The same physical event might be constructed very differently by individuals from different cultural backgrounds, highlighting the role of learned perspectives in shaping perceived reality.

Language shapes reality construction by providing categorical frameworks and conceptual structures. The words and concepts available to us influence how we parse and understand our experiences, demonstrating the deep connection between linguistic and perceptual systems.

Belief systems act as powerful filters in reality construction, affecting which interpretations we consider plausible and how we organize our understanding of events. These systems can both enhance and limit our construction of reality, depending on their flexibility and scope.

Professional expertise leads to specialized reality construction capabilities within specific domains. An architect, artist, and engineer might construct very different realities when looking at the same building, based on their training and experience.

Physical states influence reality construction through their effects on perception and processing. Fatigue, hunger, or illness can significantly alter how we construct our experience of the world, showing the embodied nature of reality construction.

Attention mechanisms guide reality construction by determining which aspects of experience receive detailed processing. These systems help manage cognitive resources while ensuring important information receives appropriate consideration.

Pattern recognition plays a vital role in reality construction by helping identify meaningful structures in complex sensory input. Our brains constantly seek and create patterns, using them to construct predictable and manageable versions of reality.

Time perception emerges from our reality construction systems, creating our experience of temporal flow. This construction involves complex integration of memory, attention, and prediction mechanisms to create our sense of past, present, and future.

Stress affects reality construction by altering attention patterns and processing priorities. Under stress, our construction systems might focus on potential threats while filtering out less survival-relevant information.

Learning processes continuously modify our reality construction systems through the integration of new information and experiences. This ongoing adaptation allows our constructed reality to become increasingly sophisticated and nuanced over time.

Social consensus influences reality construction through shared interpretations and validated experiences. Our individual constructions of reality often align with those of our social groups, creating collective understanding while maintaining personal variations.

Understanding these reality construction systems provides valuable insights into human perception and behavior. By recognizing the constructed nature of our experience, we can become more aware of our interpretive processes and potentially more flexible in our understanding of the world.

The sophistication of our reality construction systems enables us to navigate complex environments while maintaining coherent experiences. These systems support both individual functioning and social coordination, allowing us to create shared understandings while preserving unique perspectives. Their continuous operation shapes every aspect of our conscious experience, making them fundamental to human cognition and behavior.

Experience Filter Mechanisms

Experience filter mechanisms operate as sophisticated neural gatekeepers that selectively process, prioritize, and integrate incoming sensory information into our conscious awareness. These intricate systems determine which aspects of our environment receive attention and become part of our remembered experience while filtering out potentially overwhelming amounts of irrelevant data.

The primary sensory filters act as initial screening devices, processing roughly 11 million bits of information per second down to manageable streams of conscious experience. When walking through a busy street, these filters automatically prioritize relevant signals like approaching vehicles while dampening background noise from distant conversations or ambient sounds.

Emotional salience serves as a powerful filtering criterion, with the amygdala rapidly flagging emotionally significant information for enhanced processing. This evolutionary adaptation ensures that potentially important experiences receive priority attention, explaining why emotionally charged events often become our most vivid memories.

Context-dependent filters adjust their parameters based on environmental conditions and current goals. During a focused work session, these filters might suppress social media notifications while heightening attention to task-relevant information. This dynamic adjustment helps maintain appropriate focus while preserving awareness of truly important interruptions.

Social filters specifically process interpersonal cues, helping us navigate complex social situations by highlighting relevant behavioral signals while filtering out extraneous information. These mechanisms enable us to maintain meaningful conversations in noisy environments by focusing on our conversation partner's voice and expressions.

Learning-based filters develop through experience, becoming increasingly sophisticated at identifying relevant patterns and information. Expert musicians, for instance, develop highly refined auditory filters that can detect subtle variations in tone and timing that might escape untrained listeners.

Attention-driven filters respond to conscious direction while maintaining automatic background processing. When searching for a friend in a crowd, these filters enhance recognition of familiar features while reducing processing of irrelevant details, demonstrating the interaction between voluntary and involuntary filtering.

State-dependent filtering adjusts based on physical and psychological conditions. During periods of stress, these filters might become more sensitive to potential threats while decreasing attention to non-essential stimuli. Understanding these adjustments helps in managing optimal filtering conditions.

Cultural frameworks influence filter settings by establishing relevance criteria based on shared values and expectations. These culturally-shaped filters affect which experiences receive priority processing and how they are interpreted within social contexts.

Memory-linked filters compare incoming information against stored experiences, helping identify novel or significant variations that warrant attention. This comparative filtering supports both learning and survival by highlighting potentially important changes in familiar patterns.

Language-based filters process linguistic information at multiple levels, from phonetic discrimination to semantic interpretation. These sophisticated mechanisms enable us to extract meaningful communication from complex audio streams while filtering out linguistic noise.

Temporal filters manage our experience of time by selectively processing events at different temporal scales. These mechanisms explain why time seems to slow during intense experiences while passing quickly during routine activities.

Physical activity influences filter operation through its effects on arousal and attention. Regular exercise can enhance filter efficiency by improving neural circulation and maintaining optimal brain chemistry for information processing.

Sleep plays a crucial role in filter maintenance, with rest periods allowing for recalibration and optimization of filtering mechanisms. This nocturnal maintenance ensures effective filtering during waking hours while supporting memory consolidation.

Expertise development involves the refinement of domain-specific filters through sustained practice and exposure. Professional athletes, for example, develop highly specialized filters that enable rapid processing of sport-specific information while maintaining broader awareness.

Age-related changes in filtering mechanisms can affect processing efficiency, though compensatory adaptations often develop to maintain functional filtering of important information. Understanding these changes helps in developing appropriate strategies for different life stages.

Mindfulness practices can enhance conscious awareness of filtering processes, enabling more intentional control over attention and experience selection. This increased awareness supports more effective filtering while maintaining cognitive flexibility.

Environmental factors significantly influence filter operation, with different contexts requiring distinct filtering priorities. The same person might employ dramatically different filtering parameters in a library versus a concert venue.

Understanding these filtering mechanisms provides valuable insights for optimizing personal experience and performance. By recognizing how our filters operate, we can better manage our attention and create conditions that support effective information processing.

These sophisticated filtering systems form an essential part of our cognitive architecture, protecting us from information overload while ensuring important signals reach consciousness. Their continuous operation shapes every aspect of our experience, from basic perception to complex social interaction, making them fundamental to human functioning and adaptation.

Consciousness Cache Management

Consciousness cache management operates as a dynamic system that organizes and prioritizes immediate awareness, working memory, and readily accessible information. This sophisticated process determines which thoughts, sensations, and memories remain in our immediate consciousness while managing the rapid transition of information between different levels of awareness.

The primary cache system maintains a limited capacity of active thoughts and perceptions, typically holding between four to seven distinct elements at once. When you're cooking a complex meal, this cache juggles ingredient measurements, timing, and technique instructions while maintaining awareness of immediate safety concerns.

Emotional states significantly influence cache priorities, with strong feelings automatically claiming cache space and affecting the processing of other information. During moments of intense joy or anxiety, the cache becomes dominated by emotion-related content, sometimes at the expense of other cognitive tasks.

Working memory interfaces directly with the consciousness cache, providing rapid access to temporarily needed information. This interaction enables complex cognitive tasks, such as mental arithmetic or following multi-step instructions, by maintaining relevant data in an easily accessible state.

Environmental factors continuously affect cache management through sensory input prioritization. In a noisy restaurant, the cache might prioritize conversation-related information while temporarily suppressing awareness of background sounds, demonstrating dynamic adaptation to context.

Task switching requires sophisticated cache management as the system must rapidly clear and reload relevant information. When moving between different activities, the cache system coordinates the smooth transition of task-specific information while maintaining essential background awareness.

Social interactions place particular demands on cache management, requiring simultaneous tracking of conversation content, emotional signals, and social context. The cache system expertly balances these elements to support fluid social engagement while maintaining personal cognitive goals.

Learning processes depend heavily on effective cache management, as new information must be held in consciousness long enough to form lasting memories. Students utilizing active recall techniques leverage this system by repeatedly bringing information into the cache for processing.

Physical states influence cache operation, with factors like fatigue or hunger affecting capacity and efficiency. Understanding these influences helps in optimizing cache management through appropriate rest and nutrition.

Meditation practices can enhance cache management by increasing awareness of mental processes and improving control over attention allocation. Regular practitioners often report greater ability to maintain focus and manage multiple streams of consciousness effectively.

Sleep plays a crucial role in cache maintenance, with rest periods allowing for system reset and optimization. During sleep, the cache system reorganizes priorities and clears accumulated mental clutter, preparing for renewed operation upon waking.

Professional expertise develops specialized cache management patterns, enabling experts to maintain awareness of complex domain-specific information while performing related tasks. Chess masters, for instance, develop remarkable ability to hold multiple game positions in their consciousness cache simultaneously.

Time perception relates closely to cache management, as the system coordinates our experience of temporal flow through moment-to-moment awareness. The subjective speed of time often reflects how our cache manages and transitions between different states of consciousness.

Cultural factors influence cache priorities through learned patterns of attention and value assignment. These cultural effects shape which information receives priority in consciousness and how different elements are related within the cache.

Language processing requires efficient cache management to maintain coherent communication while balancing multiple linguistic elements. During conversation, the cache system coordinates grammar, vocabulary, and social context while maintaining flow of thought.

Stress affects cache operation by narrowing focus and potentially reducing effective capacity. Under pressure, the system might sacrifice broader awareness for intense focus on perceived threats or urgent tasks.

Age-related changes in cache management can affect processing efficiency, though experience often leads to compensatory strategies. Older adults frequently develop sophisticated methods for managing reduced cache capacity through improved organization and prioritization.

Physical activity can enhance cache performance by improving neural circulation and maintaining optimal brain chemistry. Regular exercise supports efficient cache management while promoting cognitive flexibility.

Understanding these cache management mechanisms provides valuable insights for optimizing mental performance. By recognizing how our consciousness cache operates, we can develop strategies to work with its natural rhythms and limitations rather than against them.

The consciousness cache system forms a crucial component of our cognitive architecture, enabling fluid thought and action while maintaining coherent experience. Its continuous operation shapes our moment-to-moment awareness, making it fundamental to human consciousness and cognitive function.